# kripalu
# seasonal
# menus

summer

from
Executive Chef
Deb Morgan

exploring the yoga of life.

# table of contents

## lunches

## dinners

## seasonal specialties

# introduction

Welcome to the first in a seasonal recipe book series from the Kripalu Kitchen. Here in the kitchen, our motto is simple: Quality. Choice. Intention. These are the cornerstones of our approach, and our vision is to support you in creating a healthy and nurturing relationship with food using these values. I invite you to bring them into your own kitchen as you experiment with these recipes and menus.

So what does "quality. choice. intention." mean to us? With every dish we create, we believe there is no substitution for quality ingredients, and quality starts with freshness. See how many of these recipes you can create from fresh, locally grown or produced ingredients. This will ensure that all of the flavors, nutritional value, and vibrant energy of the foods you cook are still intact when you eat them.

At Kripalu, choice means that there is no one way to eat that is "right" for everyone. We honor each person's knowing of what is needed for their unique body. Many of our recipes are written to accommodate everyone, with vegetarian versions or substitutions such as chicken or fish. We leave the choice to you and your family to determine what will bring you the most vitality.

Cooking with foods that are fresh and whole invites us into a profound relationship with the life-giving energy that food provides. The intention we bring to this relationship provides a key nutrient for health and vitality. Gratitude, delight, creative experiments, tastings, a desire to share with others—when we cook, our thoughts, feelings, words, and actions become powerful components of the nutritional value, flavor, and overall enjoyment of any meal.

At Kripalu, every member of our Food Service team—the people who order and receive the food, the veggie-prep team, the cooks and bakers, the servers, and the Steward team—bring a deep love for and commitment to the health of our planet and our bodies. Inspired by our passion for yoga, life, and food, we create such delicious and nourishing meals that we are regularly asked for our recipes—and our secrets. With this book, you now have both, and I sincerely hope you enjoy this beautiful presentation of our work.

May you cook—and live—with a full heart.

Executive Chef Deb Morgan
Kripalu Center for Yoga & Health

# acknowledgments

I would like to offer a special acknowledgment to the members of the Kripalu Kitchen Cook's team who have worked with these recipes to define them and bring the most out of them this season and who make walking into the Kripalu Kitchen a daily joy. In particular I want to acknowledge Kelsey Laird, my chief recipe tester in the process of scaling the recipes for home use and then preparing them for our photo shoot.

To Elena Erber and the talented marketing team: without your vision and dedication to all the details of this project, both large and small, it quite simply would not have happened. I know there will be many Kripalu guests who will be eternally grateful for your commitment. And what would a recipe book be without inspirational images? An awe-inspired thank you to Jennifer May, our photographer, for her eye for beauty and the artistry intrinsic in food, and to Jessica Bard, our food stylist, for her skillful use of tweezers and heartfelt connection to her craft.

Finally, I'd like to acknowledge Patton (Dinabandhu) and Ila Sarley. Because of their confidence and skillful support, the Kripalu Kitchen has grown into one of the country's premier natural-foods kitchens. They have been true and brilliant leaders and friends.

# how to use this book

In this book, you'll find 63 recipes from our 2010 Kripalu Kitchen summer menu. Each one has been scaled from its original quantity, which would serve 400–650 people, to a home-friendly serving size. The recipes are organized as we serve them at Kripalu, as part of an entire meal of complementary dishes, making it easy to experiment. You might try one recipe or you might plan a feast. Let yourself get creative and mix and match to design your own unique menus.

**Helpful tips for trying new recipes:**

• Read the whole recipe first so you have an understanding of everything required

• Gather all your ingredients before you begin

• Do the vegetable chopping first

• Don't be afraid to play with substitutions and additions.

This way, you'll move through the cooking and assembling stages of a recipe much more smoothly—and enjoyably.

# lunches

# lunch moroccan style

**Moroccan Chickpea Tagine • Couscous or Quinoa with Mint, Dill, and Feta • Sautéed Swiss Chard with Roasted Cinnamon Yams**

*Though tagines are traditionally prepared in a clay pot, we incorporate the concept of slow-cooking vegetables, beans, spices, and dried fruit to create this very yummy dish. Serve with couscous or quinoa and feta, add the roasted yams and Swiss chard, and you have a meal packed with nutrition and flavor. Feel free to play around with adding a meat to your tagine if you desire, as is traditional in North Africa.*

## moroccan chickpea tagine

*Serves 4*

2 tablespoons extra virgin olive oil
2 tablespoon minced garlic
1 tablespoon minced ginger
2 teaspoon cumin
2 teaspoon cinnamon
Pinch of cayenne (optional)
1 teaspoon paprika
1 large onion, medium diced
2 tablespoon tomato paste
Splash of red wine, water, or vegetable stock
2 cups small cauliflower florets
1/2 large red bell pepper, medium diced
2 stalks celery, medium diced
1 small carrot, medium diced
1 cup cooked chickpeas
1/4 cup golden raisins
1 small zucchini, sliced in half-moons
1 1/2 teaspoons salt
2 cups vegetable stock
1/4 cup toasted slivered almonds
Splash of lemon juice
4 lemon wedges

Heat the oil in a large sauté pan over medium heat. Add the garlic, ginger, cumin, cinnamon, cayenne, and paprika and stir until the spices release their fragrance. Add the onion and sauté until it begins to caramelize. Stir in the tomato paste and continue to sauté until it is thickened and slightly browned. Whisk in the splash of wine, water, or stock and stir until all browned bits have been released from the bottom of the pan.

Turn the heat up to medium-high and add in the cauliflower, peppers, celery, carrot, chickpeas, and raisins. Stir to combine and coat vegetables with the spices. Add salt and vegetable stock and simmer until the vegetables are just tender. Add the zucchini and continue to cook until the zucchini is just tender, stirring occasionally. Splash with a squeeze of lemon and stir in the toasted almonds. Serve hot with lemon wedges.

# couscous or quinoa with mint, dill, and feta

*Serves 4*

1 tablespoon minced garlic
2 cups water
1 1/2 cups couscous or 1 cup quinoa*
1 1/2 cups grape or cherry tomatoes, halved
1 1/2 cups large diced cucumber
1/2 cup sliced scallions
1/4 cup chopped mint
1/4 cup chopped dill
1/4 cup extra virgin olive oil
6 tablespoons fresh lemon juice
1 cup crumbled or diced feta cheese
1 teaspoon salt

Combine the garlic and water and bring to a boil. Turn off the heat and stir in couscous. Cover and let sit until all liquid is absorbed, about 5 minutes.

Fluff couscous with a fork and spread out on a platter to cool. Transfer couscous to a mixing bowl and toss with remaining ingredients. Serve at room temperature.

*For a gluten-free alternative, substitute roasted quinoa.

To prepare quinoa: Thoroughly rinse and drain well. Place on a baking sheet and bake at 350 degrees, turning occasionally until quinoa starts to brown, about 10 minutes. Transfer to pot with 1 3/4 cups water and bring to a boil. Simmer, covered, for 10 minutes. Remove from heat, keep covered, and let rest for 10 minutes. Fluff quinoa with a fork and spread on platter to cool. When cool, transfer quinoa to a mixing bowl and toss with remaining ingredients. Serve at room temperature.

# sautéed swiss chard with roasted cinnamon yams

*Serves 4*

1 yam or sweet potato, medium diced
2 tablespoons extra virgin olive oil
Pinch of salt
1 teaspoon cinnamon
1 bunch Swiss chard, well-rinsed and roughly chopped
2 cloves garlic, minced

Toss yam with 1 tablespoon oil, cinnamon, and a pinch of salt and spread out onto a baking sheet. Bake at 375 degrees until yam is cooked through and start to become crispy, about 10 to 20 minutes.

In a large sauté pan, heat remaining oil over medium-high heat. Add chard and garlic and sauté until tender. Add a splash of water if chard starts to stick.

Combine cooked chard with the roasted yams. Serve hot.

# a day in the life of the kripalu kitchen

From 4:00 am when our head baker arrives until 10:00 pm when the last of the compost has been taken outside by one of our enthusiastic volunteers, a staff of almost 65 dedicated people work to create and serve up to 2,000 delicious meals each day. To someone walking into our kitchens for the first time, it may appear that we are a dance troupe performing a well-choreographed routine. While our choreography is definitively important, the true magic of what takes place in the Kripalu Kitchen is all about relationship.

We strongly believe that food is a carrier of energy and that the energy of those who interact with food and the kitchen environment is a key component to the vitality a food has to offer us. So whether it's how the purchasers interact with the farmers we buy from; or how the veggie prep crew cut that 80 gallons of kale; or how the bakers mix, shape, and bake those 60 loaves of bread each day; or how the cooks stir, heat, and season 40 gallons of soup; or how the servers bring the dozens of serving trays to the buffet lines; or how the greeters welome hundreds of guests with a smile; or the how the dish crews care for the thousands of pieces of dinnerware and dozens of pots and pans; every single person and his or her energy creates the symphony that is the Kripalu dining experience. We believe it is this depth of intention that really creates the depth of flavor.

We invite you to keep this philosophy in your heart and mind as you shop, chop, stir, serve, eat, and clean up your meals. Each act is a valuable opportunity to create, share, and experience love. We can't think of a better way to enjoy food than this!

# lunch summer barbecue

**BBQ Chicken or Tofu Sandwiches ▪ Vegan Coleslaw ▪ Spring Corn Soup**

*These sandwiches are so good! The great thing is that you can make the sauce and have both the chicken and tofu prepared, ready to easily serve to your vegan and nonvegan friends. We serve these sandwiches on our sourdough Ciabatta bread with a side of Vegan Slaw and either our Spring Corn Soup or, in the summer, fresh, local corn on the cob.*

## bbq chicken or tofu sandwiches

*Serves 4*

### for the bbq sauce
2 tablespoons extra virgin olive oil
1/2 cup sliced onions
2 tablespoons minced garlic
1 tablespoon plus 1 teaspoon cumin
1/2 teaspoon ground coriander
1 teaspoon chili powder
1/2 teaspoon allspice
3 tablespoons tomato paste
Splash of red wine, water, or vegetable stock
2 tablespoons prepared brown mustard
1/4 teaspoon bottled hot sauce
2 tablespoons cider vinegar
1/3 cup molasses
1/2 cup tomato sauce
1 1/2 teaspoons salt

### for the sandwich
1 1/2 cups water
1 tablespoon extra virgin olive oil
1/2 onion, sliced
1/2 cup sliced green bell peppers
1/2 cup sliced red bell peppers
Pulled Chicken or Marinated Tofu (recipes follow)
4 warm or toasted Ciabatta bread rolls or
    your favorite rolls, split

Making the BBQ Sauce: Heat the oil in a large sauce pot over medium heat. Add the onions and garlic and sauté until they begin to caramelize. Add the cumin, coriander, chili powder, and allspice and stir until the spices release their fragrances. Stir in the tomato paste and continue to sauté until sauce becomes thickened and slightly browned. Whisk in the splash of wine, water, or stock and stir until all browned bits have been released from the bottom of the pan.

Whisk in the mustard, hot sauce, vinegar, molasses, tomato sauce, salt, and water. Simmer uncovered until sauce begins to thicken, 3 to 4 minutes.

Heat the oil in a sauté pan over medium heat. Add the onions and peppers and sauté until just softened. Add to the BBQ Sauce along with Pulled Chicken or Marinated Tofu. Use to fill each Ciabatta or roll. Serve with Vegan Coleslaw (recipe follows).

# pulled chicken

2 bone-in chicken breasts
2 bone-in chicken thighs
1/2 onion, roughly chopped
1 tablespoon salt

Combine chicken, onion, and salt in a large pot and cover with water by 1 inch. Bring to a boil, then reduce heat and simmer until chicken is cooked through. (Test with a knife to see that the meat is completely opaque.) Remove chicken and set aside to cool. (If desired, strain the broth and reserve for other uses.*) When chicken is cool enough to handle, remove the skin and pull the chicken meat off the bones, shredding it into small strips. Use as directed above for BBQ Sandwiches.

* The water the chicken was cooked in essentially becomes chicken broth. For a richer flavor, add herbs such as parsley, peppercorns, and bay leaves and vegetables such as onions, celery, and carrots along with the chicken.

# marinated tofu

1 1/2 pounds tofu
1/4 cup tamari
1/4 cup white wine

Rinse tofu well. Cut into large, matchstick-size pieces. Combine tamari and wine in a bowl and add the tofu. Add enough water to cover and gently stir. Marinate for at least one hour and up to overnight. Use as directed above for BBQ Sandwiches.

# vegan coleslaw

*Serves 4*

**for the dressing**
1/3 cup Veganaise™ (eggless mayonnaise)
2 tablespoons clover honey
1 tablespoon apple cider vinegar
1 tablespoon fresh lemon juice
1/2 teaspoon celery seed
1/2 teaspoon sea salt
Pinch of black pepper

**for the salad**
1 cup shredded green cabbage
1 cup shredded red cabbage
1/2 cup grated carrots

Combine dressing ingredients in a large bowl and mix well. Fold in the cabbage and carrots. Chill before serving.

# spring corn soup

*Serves 4*

2 tablespoons Earth Balance™
 (non-hydrogenated vegan spread)
1 small onion, medium diced
1 leek, white and light green part, thinly sliced or diced
1 small carrot, diced
1 stalk celery, diced
1/2 zucchini, medium diced
1/2 yellow squash, medium diced
2 cups fresh or frozen corn kernels
6 cups vegetable stock
2 tablespoons chopped dill
1 teaspoon sea salt
Pinch of black pepper
1/2 tablespoon apple cider vinegar
1/4 cup chopped cilantro (optional)

Heat the Earth Balance in a soup pot over medium heat. Add the onions, leeks, carrots, and celery and sauté until tender. Stir in the zucchini, squash, corn, stock, dill, salt, and pepper. Simmer until vegetables are just tender, being careful not to overcook them. Just before serving, stir in the vinegar. If desired, garnish each serving with cilantro.

# lunch an oriental occasion

**Tofu and Vegetables in Coconut-Ginger Sauce • Jasmine Rice • Vegetable Egg Rolls • Sweet Ginger Sauce**

*The coconut milk gives this vegan dish its delicious richness and yet keeps it light enough for a wonderful spring or summer occasion. For a fun side we serve our Vegetable Egg Rolls, baking them to keep the oil content lower than the traditional deep-frying method. Dipped in our homemade Sweet Ginger Sauce, they can be a meal in themselves.*

## tofu and vegetables in coconut-ginger sauce

*Serves 4*

1 pound firm tofu, cut into large cubes
1 cup water
1/2 cup white wine
1 1/2 teaspoons salt
2 tablespoons coconut oil
1 tablespoon minced garlic
2 tablespoons minced ginger
1/2 teaspoon chili flakes (optional)
2 tablespoons minced lemongrass
1 small onion, sliced
1 small carrot, sliced
1 small zucchini, sliced
1 1/2 cups coconut milk
1 tablespoon arrowroot
3/4 cup well-drained, cubed pineapple
1 cup snow peas
1 teaspoon fresh lime juice
Cilantro to garnish (optional)

Marinate the tofu cubes overnight in the water, wine, and 1/2 teaspoon salt. (If you do not have time to marinate overnight, heat the water, wine, and 1/2 teaspoon salt and pour over the tofu. Let sit while you prepare the rest of the ingredients.) Drain well before using.

Heat the coconut oil in a large sauté pan. Add the garlic, ginger, half the chili flakes, if using, and lemongrass and lightly sauté for 2 to 3 minutes. Add the onion, carrot, and remaining salt and sauté until vegetables are tender.

Add the coconut milk and the drained tofu. Bring to a simmer and cook until tofu is warmed through, about 10 minutes.

Mix the arrowroot with 2 tablespoons cold water. Bring the vegetables and coconut milk mixture to a boil and slowly stir in the arrowroot mixture. Stir until thickened. Add the zucchini, pineapple, and snow peas. Reduce heat and simmer just until zucchini and snow peas begin to soften. Stir in lime juice. Garnish with cilantro and remaining chili flakes, if using, and serve with Jasmine Rice (recipe follows).

## jasmine rice

*Makes 4 cups*

3 cups water
2 cups jasmine rice
Pinch of salt

Rinse rice well and drain. In a sauce pan with a tight-fitting lid, bring water and rice to a boil. Add salt and reduce heat to low. Cover and simmer until all water is absorbed, about 15 minutes. Turn off heat and let sit, covered, for 5 minutes before serving.

# vegetable egg rolls

*Makes 8*

8 egg roll wrappers
2 tablespoons sesame oil
1 1/2 tablespoons minced garlic
1 1/2 tablespoons minced ginger
2 cups matchstick or shredded carrots
1 small onion, thinly sliced
1 cup sliced mushrooms
2 cups thinly sliced green cabbage
1/2 cup small matchstick daikon radish (optional)
1 tablespoon tamari
1 teaspoon toasted sesame oil
Squeeze of lime juice
Sweet Ginger Sauce (recipe follows)

Heat the 2 tablespoons sesame oil in a sauté pan over medium heat. Add the ginger and garlic and sauté for a few minutes. Increase heat and add the carrots, onions, mushrooms, cabbage, and daikon, if using, and continue to sauté until vegetables are tender but not too soft. Turn heat off and stir in tamari, toasted sesame oil, and a squeeze of lime juice. Transfer to a platter to cool. (This filling can be made a day ahead.)

Then follow the diagram on the back of the egg roll wrapper package to roll filling inside wrappers.

The egg rolls can be fried in deep oil, pan-fried in shallow oil, or baked. To bake, place the egg rolls on an oiled baking sheet and spray or rub a thin coat of oil on the outside of each roll. Bake at 375 degrees for 15 minutes, turning every 5 minutes until the outside of wrapper begins to crisp.

Serve with Sweet Ginger Sauce.

# sweet ginger sauce

*Makes 1 1/2 cups*

1 cup water
1/2 cup dried, pitted apricots
2 dried, pitted prunes, chopped
2 teaspoons orange juice
2 teaspoons minced ginger
1 teaspoon brown rice vinegar
1/2 teaspoon salt
1 tablespoon honey

Combine all ingredients except honey in a small pot. Simmer for 10 minutes. Stir in honey. Cool slightly. Transfer to a blender and puree until smooth.

# lunch from the middle east

**Lebanese Tomato Rice Soup · Roasted Cauliflower · Tahini Sauce · Charmoula Sauce**

*If you have never tried roasting cauliflower, you will be delighted by both the ease of preparation as well as the wonderful results. Try it topped with either of these sauces. We serve this meal with traditional falafel and pita bread as well as this amazing tomato soup.*

## lebanese tomato rice soup

*Serves 6–8*

3 tablespoons extra virgin olive oil
1 medium onion, medium diced
5 cloves garlic, minced
2 large tomatoes, medium diced
1 32-ounce can of tomato puree
4 cups vegetable stock
1/4 cup uncooked basmati rice, rinsed and drained
1/2 teaspoon sea salt
3/4 cup chopped mint
3 tablespoon fresh lemon juice

Heat the oil in a soup pot over medium-low heat. Add the onions and garlic and gently sauté until translucent. Add the tomatoes and sauté a few minutes. Add the tomato puree, stock, rice, and salt. Bring to a boil, then turn down to a low heat and simmer for 20 minutes until the rice is cooked. Add mint and lemon juice and simmer for 5 minutes. Taste for flavor and adjust with salt or lemon juice if needed.

## roasted cauliflower

*Serves 4*

1 head cauliflower, cut into medium florets
2 tablespoons extra virgin olive oil
Pinch of salt
Parsley for garnish (optional)

Toss cauliflower with olive oil and a pinch of salt and place in a baking pan. Add 1/2 inch of water and cover with foil. Bake at 350 degrees until cauliflower begins to soften, about 20 minutes. Uncover cauliflower and continue to bake so that the top begins to brown. Garnish with chopped parsley or top with Tahini or Charmoula sauce (recipes follow).

Note: For a beautiful presentation, try baking the cauliflower whole. Remove any outer leaves, slice across the bottom of the cauliflower to create a flat surface, and place in a baking pan as above. Baking time will vary depending on size of the cauliflower, but will be about 45 minutes. Present at the table on a platter with one or both sauces.

# tahini sauce

*Makes 1 cup*

1/2 cup sesame tahini
1/4 cup water
1/3 to 1/2 cup fresh lemon juice
2 cloves garlic, minced
1 teaspoon chopped parsley (optional)
1/2 teaspoon sea salt

Combine all ingredients in a bowl and whisk together or place in a blender jar and puree. Adjust consistency with water. Serve with Roasted Cauliflower or use as a dip for pita bread.

# charmoula sauce

*Makes 2 cups*

3/4 cup chopped cilantro leaves and stems (well-rinsed)
3/4 cup chopped parsley leaves and stems (well-rinsed)
2/3 cup extra virgin olive oil
1/3 cup fresh lemon juice
1/4 cup water
1 tablespoon minced garlic
1 teaspoon cumin
1/2 teaspoon paprika
1/2 teaspoon sea salt

Combine all ingredients in the bowl of a food processor. Pulse until well combined. Serve with Roasted Cauliflower.

healthy living note
# local and loving it
Kathie Madonna Swift, nutritionist

*In matters of taste, consider nutrition. In matters of nutrition, consider taste.* —Julia Child

Julia Child surely must have been referring to "eating locally grown" when she coined this famous phrase. There are no better flavors than those from good, healthy produce and provisions. Due to increased interest and awareness, community gardens and farmer's markets can be found just about everywhere, including at rest stops on major highways and in urban areas. Michel Nischan, chef and author of *Sustainably Delicious*, considers eating locally grown a healthy act of heroism. Eating local not only reduces our carbon footprint, it supports a sustainable food system. And, as Julia would surely have agreed, locally grown food simply tastes better.

Summer is a perfect time to adventure out and discover the many edible delights bursting with nutritional goodness in every bite. To help you in your quest for local fare, there are a number of resources available online, including www.localharvest.org and www.farmfresh.org, that can lead you in the right direction.

# lunch fire up the grill

**Cheddar-Stuffed Turkey Burgers ▪ Portabella and Goat Cheese Burgers ▪ Roasted Red Pepper Vegan Aioli ▪ Basil and Caper Vegan Aioli ▪ Roasted Red Potato Salad**

*Every spring and summer in our menu rotation we traditionally serve burgers to inspire a feeling of the grilling season. This year we set about to create turkey and vegetarian versions that would wow everyone into burger bliss. Both of these stuffed burgers do that for me, topped with either of our vegan "aioli" sauces and served with our red potato salad and a fresh piece of corn on the cob. I hope you'll agree.*

## cheddar-stuffed turkey burgers

*Makes 6*

1 small Spanish onion, medium diced
3 tablespoons extra virgin olive oil
1/2 cup chopped fresh basil
1 1/2 pounds ground turkey meat
1 1/2 teaspoons sea salt
1/2 teaspoon black pepper
2 teaspoons Worcestershire sauce
1/2 cup Panko or other bread crumbs
3/4 cup grated cheddar cheese
1 teaspoon bottled hot sauce
6 whole wheat buns, split

Heat 1 tablespoon oil in a small sauté pan over medium heat. Add onions and sauté until caramelized. Set aside to cool.

In a large bowl, blend basil with remaining oil. Add the turkey, 1 teaspoon salt, pepper, and the Worcestershire sauce and mix well. Set aside.

In another bowl, combine the caramelized onions, bread crumbs, cheese, hot sauce, and remaining 1/2 teaspoon salt.

Divide turkey into six equal balls. Stuff each ball with a sixth of the cheese mixture and then form into patties.

Bake burgers at 350 degrees for about 20 minutes; you may also grill or fry them. Serve burgers on whole wheat buns with Basil and Caper Vegan Aioli or Roasted Red Pepper Vegan Aioli (recipes follow).

# portabella and goat cheese burgers

*Makes 6*

2 tablespoons extra virgin olive oil
5 cups chopped portabella mushrooms
1 cup medium diced Spanish onion
1 1/2 cups small diced red bell pepper
2 tablespoons chopped shallot
2 tablespoons chopped fresh thyme
2 tablespoons white wine
1 teaspoon sea salt
Pinch black pepper
2 cups toasted pecans
1 cup pecan meal (finely ground pecans, not a paste)
1/2 cup white rice flour
1/3 cup fresh goat cheese (chevre)
1/4 cup chopped fresh parsley
6 whole wheat buns, split

Heat the olive oil in a large sauté pan. Add the portabella mushrooms, onions, red pepper, shallots, and thyme and sauté until the vegetables are just tender. Add the wine, salt, and pepper. Remove from heat and let cool.

Put the toasted pecans in the bowl of a food processor. Pulse a few times just to break them up. Add 3/4 of the cooled vegetable mixture and pulse until just combined; do not over blend to create mush. Transfer to a mixing bowl. Fold in the pecan meal and rice flour. Gently fold in the remaining 1/4 of the vegetables, goat cheese, and parsley. Form into 6 patties.

Bake on an oiled baking tray at 350 degrees until burgers are warmed through, about 15 minutes. Serve burgers on whole wheat buns with Basil and Caper Vegan Aioli or Roasted Red Pepper Vegan Aioli (recipes follow).

# roasted red pepper vegan aioli

*Makes about 3/4 cup*

1 red bell pepper
4 cloves garlic
1/8 teaspoon salt
Pinch black pepper
1/2 teaspoon bottled hotsauce
1/2 cup Veganaise™ (eggless mayonnaise)
Juice of 1/2 lemon

Place the bell pepper directly on the rack in a 400 degree oven. Place the garlic cloves in a foil pouch and place in the oven. Roast until the bell pepper turns very dark with spots of black on the outside. Remove the garlic when you remove the bell pepper. Place the pepper in a bowl and cover tightly so that steam is created. When it has cooled enough to handle, remove the skin and seeds. Remove the skin from the garlic.

Combine the roasted bell pepper and garlic in the bowl of a food processor. Puree until smooth. Transfer to a mixing bowl. Gently mix in remaining ingredients.

# basil and caper vegan aioli

*Makes about 1 cup*

3/4 cup Veganaise™ (eggless mayonnaise)
1 tablespoon fresh lemon juice
2 cloves garlic, minced
1 tablespoon capers
1 bunch fresh basil, well-rinsed and dried

Combine the Veganaise, lemon juice, garlic, and capers in a mixing bowl.

Very finely chop the basil and gently fold into the Veganaise mixture.

# roasted red potato salad

*Serves 4–6*

**for the salad**
4 cups cubed red potatoes
2 teaspoons extra virgin olive oil
Pinch of sea salt
1 cup cut green beans (about 1 inch long)
1/4 red onion, sliced

**for the dressing**
2 tablespoons extra virgin olive oil
1 tablespoon red wine vinegar
1 tablespoon Dijon mustard
1 tablespoon chopped rosemary
Sea salt and black pepper, to taste

Toss the potatoes with the olive oil and salt. Place on a baking sheet. Roast in a 375 degree oven until tender, about 20 minutes depending on the size of your cubes. Set aside to cool.

Steam the green beans until tender. Cool.

In a large bowl, whisk together the dressing ingredients. Fold in the potatoes, green beans, and red onions. This potato salad may be served right away, slightly warmed or cooled.

# lunch a flavorful twist on soup and a sandwich

**Broccoli-Cheddar Turnovers · Vegan Mediterranean Turnovers · Summer Minestrone**

*If you have been fortunate enough to spend an extended amount of time at Kripalu, you know that turnovers (also called empanadas) are a biweekly treat that we love. This season's fillings offer two versions: the all-time favorite combination of broccoli and cheddar cheese (we recommend using raw, sharp cheddar if available) and a vegan version so packed with flavor you'll be torn about claiming one as your favorite. We serve ours with this light and tasty Summer Minestrone.*

## broccoli-cheddar turnovers

*Makes 6–7*

1 tablespoon ghee (clarified butter) or regular
   butter
1 cup large diced onion
Pinch of nutmeg
3 cups small broccoli florets
1 1/2 cups grated sharp cheddar cheese
3/4 teaspoon sea salt
1/4 teaspoon black pepper
Turnover (Empanada) Dough (recipe follows)

Heat the ghee or butter in a sauté pan over medium-high heat. Add the onions and sauté until caramelized. Add the nutmeg and set aside to cool.

Blanch the broccoli, leaving it still tender-crisp. (Be careful not to overcook.) Set aside to cool.

In a large mixing bowl, combine onions, broccoli, cheese, salt, and pepper.

Fill dough as directed (recipe on next page).

## vegan mediterranean turnovers

*Makes 6–7*

2 tablespoons extra virgin olive oil
1 small onion, small diced
3 tablespoons minced garlic
1 cup medium diced eggplant (not peeled)
1 cup small diced red bell pepper
1/4 cup sun-dried tomatoes (soaked in hot water
   for 5 minutes if needed, then sliced)
1 teaspoon sea salt
1/2 cup toasted, chopped almonds
1/4 cup chopped fresh basil
1 tablespoon red wine vinegar
2 teaspoons balsamic vinegar
1/4 teaspoon black pepper
Turnover (Empanada) Dough (recipe follows)

Heat the oil in a sauté pan over medium-high heat. Add the onions and garlic and sauté until starting to brown. Add the eggplant, red bell pepper, sun-dried tomatoes, and salt and sauté until tender. Stir in almonds, basil, vinegars, and pepper. Set aside to cool.

Use as filling for Turnover (Empanada) Dough (recipe on next page).

27

# turnover (empanada) dough

*Makes 6–7*

1 1/2 cups unbleached all-purpose flour
1 1/2 cups whole wheat pastry flour
2 teaspoons sea salt
1 3/4 cups non-hydrogenated palm shortening
1/2 cup cold water

In a mixing bowl, combine the flours and salt. Cut the shortening into pea-sized pieces. Using your hands or a food processor, work the shortening into the flour until mixture is crumbly (some larger pieces of shortening is fine). Add the water, tossing and kneading a bit to mix well. Refrigerate for 1 hour before rolling.

On a lightly floured work surface, roll out the dough fairly thin about 1/8-inch thick. Cut into 6 or 7 6-inch circles. (You may need to roll out scraps of dough to get final circles.)

Place 1/3 cup of filling on one side of each dough circle and fold over. Pinch or crimp the edges to seal. Bake at 425 degrees until crust is golden and flaky, 15 to 20 minutes.

# summer minestrone

*Serves 4*

1/2 cup dried cannellini beans (or 1 15.5-oz
   can cannellini beans, drained)
1 inch kombu seaweed
1 dry bay leaf
1/4 pound brown rice elbow pasta
2 tablespoons extra virgin olive oil, plus
   more to garnish
1 small onion, medium diced
2 tablespoons garlic, minced
2 stalks celery, medium diced
1 small carrot, medium diced
2 tablespoons tomato paste
Splash of wine, water, or stock
1 tomato, chopped

1/2 cup cut green beans (about 1 inch long)
1/2 zucchini, medium diced
1/2 yellow squash, medium diced
6 cups vegetable stock
2 tablespoons chopped fresh rosemary
1 teaspoon sea salt
1 cup baby spinach
Pinch of pepper
Chopped fresh basil (optional)

If using dried beans, soak them for at least 4 hours but preferably overnight and then cook beans with kombu and bay leaf until tender. Season to taste with salt.

Cook the pasta in boiling water until just tender. Drain and rinse in cold water. Set aside to cool.

Heat oil in a large soup pot over medium heat. Add onion and garlic and sauté until they begin to caramelize. Add celery and carrots and continue to sauté until they are just tender. Stir in the tomato paste and continue to sauté until it is thickened and slightly browned. Whisk in the splash of wine, water, or stock and stir until all browned bits have been released from the bottom of the pan.

Add the cooked beans, tomatoes, green beans, zucchini, yellow squash, stock, rosemary, salt, and pepper. Simmer for 10 minutes.

Stir in the spinach and pasta. Taste soup and adjust flavor with salt and pepper. Serve hot, drizzled with extra virgin olive oil and chopped basil if desired.

# dinners

# dinner with a tropical touch

**Walnut-Coconut-Encrusted Chicken or Tempeh ▪ Mango-Ginger Sauce ▪ Roasted Millet with Fresh Mint ▪ Bib Salad with Papaya Dressing**

*Topped with the Mango-Ginger Sauce, the taste of this crispy coconut chicken or tempeh combines everything there is to love about food. It's sweet, salty, spicy, crunchy, tender, and yummy. The papaya dressing over salad greens with pepitas and peppers creates a light and tropical meal.*

## walnut-coconut-encrusted chicken or tempeh

*Serves 4*

2 boneless, skinless chicken breasts,
    or 1 1/2 8-ounce packages tempeh
2 cups toasted walnuts, roughly chopped
2 1/2 cups toasted, unsweetened coconut
1 teaspoon sea salt
1/2 teaspoon black pepper
1/4 cup Dijon mustard
3 tablespoons agave syrup
2 tablespoons tamari (only if using tempeh)
Mango-Ginger Sauce (recipe follows)

If using chicken, butterfly the chicken breasts in half lengthwise to make 4 pieces. Pound each breast lightly to an even thickness.

If using tempeh, cut into finger-sized pieces. Steam for 5 minutes. Transfer to a shallow pan and toss with the tamari and enough water to cover. Cover and marinate at least 4 hours or overnight.

Place walnuts in the bowl of a food processor. Pulse until finely ground (but not too powdery). Transfer to a mixing bowl. Stir in the coconut, salt, and pepper. Set aside.

In a shallow bowl, combine the mustard and agave syrup. Set aside.

Dip each piece of chicken or marinated tempeh into the mustard mixture, coating both sides, then into the walnut-coconut mixture, coating both sides. Place pieces onto an oiled baking sheet. Bake at 350 degrees until cooked through, 25 to 30 minutes, depending on thickness of your chicken or the size of your tempeh. Serve hot with Mango-Ginger Sauce (recipe follows).

# mango-ginger sauce

*Makes about 3 cups*

2 1/2 cups chopped mango (fresh or frozen, thawed)
5 tablespoons fresh lime juice
3 tablespoons minced ginger
1 teaspoon minced garlic
1 teaspoon toasted cumin seeds
1 teaspoon honey
1 jalapeño, minced
1/2 teaspoon hot sauce
1/2 teaspoon sea salt

Combine all ingredients in the bowl of a food processor or a blender. Puree until smooth. Serve cold or at room temperature.

# roasted millet with fresh mint

*Serves 4*

1 cup millet
2 1/2 cups water
2 tablespoons extra virgin olive oil
2 tablespoons minced fresh mint
2 tablespoons chopped scallions
Pinch of salt and black pepper

Rinse millet well and place on a baking tray and bake at 350 degrees, stirring every few minutes, until millet starts to turn golden-brown, about 12 minutes.

Place roasted millet in a pot with the water and bring to a boil, then let simmer for 20 minutes until millet is soft. Add remaining ingredients and fluff with a fork. Serve immediately.

# bib lettuce with papaya dressing

*Serves 4*

**for the dressing**
1 1/2 cups cubed fresh papaya
1 tablespoon plus 2 teaspoons papaya seeds
1 tablespoon plus 1 teaspoon red wine vinegar
2 cloves garlic, minced
1/8 teaspoon sea salt
2 tablespoons chopped fresh basil
1/2 cup water
2 tablespoons fresh lemon juice
Pinch of black pepper
1 teaspoon honey
1 1/2 cups extra virgin olive oil

**for the salad**
6 cups torn Boston lettuce leaves
1/4 cup toasted pumpkin seeds (pepitas)
1/2 red bell pepper, medium diced

Put all dressing ingredients except the olive oil in the jar of a blender. Puree until smooth. With the motor running, very slowly drizzle in the olive oil. The dressing will be thick and emulsified.

Combine the lettuce, pumpkin seeds, and bell pepper in a salad bowl. Add some of the dressing and toss to coat the lettuce. Add more if desired. Serve immediately.

healthy living note
# food as medicine
Susan Lord, MD

Western medicine teaches us that good food is the basis for good health. Food has the power to prevent much of the chronic illnesses we experience today and can play a critical part in treating these illnesses in a safe and more balancing way than pharmaceuticals alone. Eating a fresh, whole-foods diet is a very different experience from eating things that have no nutritional value, many of which have properties that can hurt us. Plant-based foods are particularly nourishing and healing as they supply us with nutrients and energy on many levels.

Food nourishes more than our bodies, it nourishes our souls and provides us with cultural meaning. Throughout history, meals have been a natural setting for people to come together. Our religious ceremonies often involve food. It is through food that we love and nourish our babies. Food brings prana, or life force, into our bodies, where it is transformed into energy to sustain us as people living authentic, meaningful lives who serve our communities as much as ourselves. Food touches the deepest levels of who we are as human beings, inviting health and wholeness.

# dinner from south america with love

**Peruvian Rice with Shrimp or Smoked Tofu · Peruvian Tomato Salad**

*Our Senior Sous Chef at Kripalu, Michael Pigott, has an intimate connection with Peru. Each year when he returns from a trip, he brings back native ideas for delicious dinners. This Peruvian rice with shrimp is so simple to make yet so wonderful to eat. The smoked tofu version is ours, but no less tantalizing. Serve with the tomato salad and Passion Punch, one of our signature drinks (see page 56), on a warm summer evening.*

## peruvian rice with shrimp or smoked tofu

*Serves 4*

1 cup basmati rice
2 cups water or vegetable stock
1 tablespoon extra virgin olive oil
1/2 onion, small diced
1 clove garlic
2 teaspoons cumin
1 small carrot, small diced
1 bunch cilantro, well-rinsed, leaves and
   stems chopped
2 teaspoons minced Amarillo chili pepper
   (or 2 teaspoons chili pepper flakes)
1/2 cup vegetable stock (or seafood stock,
   if you like)
1 teaspoon sea salt
1/4 teaspoon black pepper
1/2 cup frozen peas
1/2 pound large shrimp, peeled and de-veined, or
   1 1/2 cups smoked tofu, cut into small cubes
   (available at gourmet and natural-foods stores)

Rinse and drain the rice. Place in a sauce pot with 2 cups water or stock. Bring to a boil, reduce heat to low, and cover. Simmer until all the water is absorbed, about 20 minutes. Let rest, covered, for 5 minutes, then fluff with a fork. Set aside.

Heat olive oil in a deep-sided sauté pan over medium heat. Add onion and garlic and sauté until just starting to brown. Add carrots and cumin and sauté until carrots are tender. Add most of the cilantro (reserving some for garnish), Amarillo chili pepper, 1/2 cup stock, salt, and pepper. Simmer for 5 minutes.

Meanwhile, season the shrimp with a little salt and pepper and give it a quick sear on a hot griddle or in a sauté pan with a little olive oil. Then add seared shrimp (or tofu, if using) to the rice and gently stir in the sauté mixture plus the peas. Keep on heat until everything is warmed through. Serve hot.

## peruvian tomato salad

*Serves 4*

4 plum tomatoes, seeded and cut into julienne
   strips
1 red onion, cut into julienne strips
1 bunch cilantro, well-rinsed and chopped
2 tablespoons extra virgin olive oil
2 to 3 tablespoons lime juice to taste
1/2 teaspoon sea salt
1 teaspoon Amarillo chili pepper (or 1 teaspoon
   chili pepper flakes)

Combine all ingredients. Cover and let marinate for at least 1 hour in the refrigerator before serving.

35

# dinner flavors of italy

**Chicken Italiano · White Bean and Tempeh Italiano · Roasted Garlic and Basil Polenta · Green Salad with Roasted Beets and Goat Cheese**

*The flavors that pop out of both the Chicken Italiano and our White Bean and Tempeh Italiano will enliven anyone you serve this to. Served with homemade polenta and a salad featuring roasted beets and soft goat cheese, this meal promises to be a family favorite.*

## chicken italiano

*Serves 4*

2 boneless, skinless chicken breasts
1/2 cup plus 2 tablespoons white wine
2 teaspoons sea salt
2 tablespoons extra virgin olive oil
1 large onion, sliced
4 cloves garlic, minced
1/2 cup canned artichoke hearts, quartered
3 tablespoons sliced sun-dried tomatoes (soaked in hot water for 5 minutes if needed to hydrate)
1/4 cup chopped fresh basil
Splash of fresh lemon juice
Roasted Garlic and Basil Polenta (recipe follows)

Butterfly the chicken breasts in half lengthwise to make 4 pieces. Place in a shallow dish and add 1/2 cup white wine, 1 teaspoon salt, and enough water to cover. Cover and let marinate for at least 1 hour in the refrigerator; chicken can marinate up to 4 hours.

Heat oil in a large sauté pan over medium heat. Add onions and garlic and sauté until onions are caramelized. Add the artichoke hearts, sun-dried tomatoes, and basil. Simmer gently for 10 minutes.

Season the chicken breasts with salt and pepper and place on an oiled baking sheet and bake at 350 degrees until just cooked through, 10 to 12 minutes. (Be careful not to overcook.) Place cooked chicken in sauté pan and toss sauce over chicken pieces and allow to simmer 2 to 3 minutes. Serve the chicken topped with the sauce over Roasted Garlic and Basil Polenta.

## white bean and tempeh italiano

*Serves 4*

1 8-ounce package of tempeh, cut into small cubes
3 tablespoons extra virgin olive oil
2 tablespoons Bragg Liquid Aminos™ (all-purpose seasoning) or tamari
1 large onion, medium diced
3 cloves garlic, minced
3 tablespoons sliced sun-dried tomatoes (soaked in hot water for 5 minutes if needed to hydrate)
1/2 cup canned artichoke hearts, quartered
2 tablespoons white wine
1/4 cup chopped fresh basil
1 15.5-ounce can cannellini beans or 1 3/4 cup cooked beans, drained
1/2 teaspoon sea salt

Combine the tempeh, 2 tablespoons oil, and the Bragg Liquid Aminos or tamari in a mixing bowl. Toss together and transfer to a baking sheet. Bake at 350 degrees until a little crispy on the outside, about 20 minutes. Set aside.

In a large sauté pan, heat the remaining tablespoon of oil and sauté onion and garlic until tender. Add the sun-dried tomatoes, artichoke hearts, wine, half the basil, beans, and salt. Simmer gently for 15 minutes. Add the roasted tempeh and simmer until heated through. Stir in remaining basil and serve hot.

# roasted garlic and basil polenta

*Serves 4–6*

4 cloves garlic, peeled
1 tablespoon extra virgin olive oil
1 cup coarse ground cornmeal
3 3/4 cups cold water
1/4 cup chopped fresh basil

Toss garlic with oil and place in a small baking dish. Roast at 350 degrees for 10 minutes. Remove from oven and mash the garlic.

Combine the garlic, cornmeal, water, and basil in a large sturdy pot and bring to a boil. Reduce the heat and simmer, stirring often, until cornmeal is tender and has thickened. This will take approximately 45 minutes. Add additional water if polenta becomes too thick but is not yet cooked through. Serve hot, garnished with basil (optional).

# green salad with roasted beets and goat cheese

*Serves 4–6*

2 cups medium diced, peeled beets
3 tablespoons extra virgin olive oil
1/2 teaspoon sea salt plus more to taste
6 cups organic green leaf lettuce and/or a
   spring mix
1 teaspoon red wine vinegar
2 tablespoons fresh fennel fronds
1/3 cup crumbled, fresh goat cheese

Toss beets with 2 tablespoons oil and 1/2 teaspoon salt. Roast at 375 degrees until tender, about 20 minutes. Cool.

Toss salad greens with the remaining tablespoon of oil, vinegar, fennel fronds, and a pinch of salt. Transfer to a serving dish and top with the cooled beets and goat cheese.

# dinner delightfully vegetarian

**Seitan Burgundy ▪ Roasted Quinoa with Cumin ▪ Kale with Roasted Cherry Tomatoes**

*This is one of those meals that surprises many of our nonvegetarian guests. With the sweetness and saltiness of the sauce on vegetarian seitan (made from wheat gluten) and the succulence of the roasted vegetables, even nonvegetarians will feel delightfully satisfied. It pairs nicely with our roasted quinoa and a side of sautéed kale and cherry tomatoes.*

## seitan burgundy

*Serves 4*

2 cups cubed seitan (1 pound of cubed
   tofu may be substituted)
1 cup button mushrooms
1/2 cup frozen pearl onions
1 carrot, cut into 1-inch cubes
1 parsnip, cut into 1-inch cubes
2 tablespoons extra virgin olive oil,
   more if needed
2 cups vegetable stock or water
2 tablespoons Earth Balance™ (non-
   hydrogenated vegan spread) or butter
3 tablespoons minced garlic
1/2 cup red Burgundy wine
2 tablespoons tomato paste
2 tablespoons chopped fresh thyme
1 teaspoon sea salt
1/2 teaspoon black pepper

Preheat oven to 400 degrees. Toss the following in separate bowls, each with a little olive oil, salt, and pepper: seitan, mushrooms, onions, carrots, and parsnips. Place each group on a baking sheet and roast until each vegetable group is tender and the seitan is a little crispy on the outside. Timing will vary depending on the size of your vegetables. Remove each from the oven as it is done and set aside.

In a large sauté pan, combine stock or water, Earth Balance or butter, garlic, wine, tomato paste, thyme, salt, and pepper in a stewpot. Simmer over medium heat for 10 minutes.

When all vegetables and seitan are roasted, toss into sauce and simmer for at least 5 minutes before serving.

Serve hot with Roasted Quinoa with Cumin and Kale with Roasted Cherry Tomatoes (recipes follow).

# roasted quinoa with cumin

*Serves 4*

1 cup quinoa
1 3/4 cups vegetable stock or water
1 tablespoon cumin seeds
Pinch of sea salt
1/4 cup chopped cilantro

Thoroughly rinse the quinoa and drain well. Place on a baking sheet and bake at 350 degrees, turning occasionally until quinoa starts to brown, about 10 minutes. Transfer the quinoa to a pot and add the stock (or water) and salt.

Place cumin seeds in a dry skillet. Turn heat to medium and toast the seeds, stirring often until cumin becomes fragrant and lightly toasted, 1 to 2 minutes.

Add the toasted cumin seeds to the quinoa mixture. Bring to a boil, reduce heat, and cover. Simmer for 10 minutes. Remove from heat, keep covered, and let rest for 10 minutes. Fluff with a fork and stir in the cilantro before serving.

# kale with roasted cherry tomatoes

*Serve 4*

1 cup cherry tomatoes
2 tablespoons extra virgin olive oil
1/4 teaspoon sea salt
1/2 teaspoon black pepper
4 cups chopped kale (any variety; we use
    stemmed curly leaf or lacinato/cavalo nero)
1 cup water

Toss the cherry tomatoes with 1 tablespoon oil, salt, and pepper. Place on a baking sheet and roast at 350 degrees until they have softened and the skins crinkle, 12 to 15 minutes. Set aside.

Combine kale and water in a large sauté pan and bring to a boil. Reduce heat to low, cover, and steam until kale is tender and most of the water has evaporated.

Toss kale with roasted tomatoes and the remaining tablespoon of oil. Serve hot.

# dinner mediterranean nights

**Mediterranean Halibut or Tempeh · Asparagus Risotto · Spinach and Swiss Chard with Pine Nuts · Crostini with Romesco and White Bean Spread**

*Our Mediterranean Halibut or Tempeh makes for such a wonderful meal. It is simple and full of fresh flavors. We serve ours over asparagus risotto with a side of spinach and pine nuts. To make the crostini, simply slice a baquette, toss with a little olive oil and salt, and bake until crispy. They are great topped with our Romesco or White Bean Spread.*

## mediterranean halibut or tempeh

*Serves 4*

**for the marinade**
1/4 cup white wine
2 tablespoons fresh lemon juice
2 tablespoons extra virgin olive oil
1/4 teaspoon sea salt
Pinch of black pepper

**for the halibut or tempeh**
1 pound halibut (or haddock)
    or 1 1/2 8-ounce package tempeh
1 tablespoon extra virgin olive oil
1 large Spanish onion, medium diced
3 cloves garlic, minced
1 cup canned tomato puree
1 medium tomato, medium diced
1 bay leaf
1 teaspoon white wine vinegar
1 teaspoon fresh lemon juice
1/2 teaspoon orange zest
3 tablespoons orange juice
1 teaspoon fennel seed
1 tablespoon minced fresh oregano
1/2 tablespoon minced fresh thyme,
    plus more for garnish
1 tablespoon minced fresh basil,
    plus more for garnish
1/2 teaspoon sea salt

If using tempeh, begin by cutting tempeh into your desired shape (cubes or small triangles work well). Steam tempeh for 5 minutes before proceeding with recipe.

Combine marinade ingredients and pour over the fish or tempeh in a shallow dish. Cover and marinate the fish for 1 hour, the tempeh for 4 hours or overnight.

Heat olive oil in a large sauté pan over medium heat. Add the onions and garlic and sauté until onions begin to brown. Stir in the remaining ingredients and simmer for 15 minutes.

Remove the fish or tempeh from the marinade and place in a baking pan. Pour the sauce over the fish or tempeh. Cover with foil and bake at 375 degrees until fish is cooked through or tempeh is thoroughly warmed, about 12 to 15 minutes depending on the thickness of the fish. Garnish with basil and thyme. Serve hot with Asparagus Risotto and Spinach and Swiss Chard with Pine Nuts (recipes follow).

# asparagus risotto

*Serves 4*

1 teaspoon saffron threads
4 cups vegetable stock
1/4 cup Earth Balance™ (non-hydrogenated
    vegan spread)
1/2 onion, medium diced
2 cloves garlic, minced
1 teaspoon dry basil
2 sprigs fresh thyme
1 teaspoon sea salt
2 bay leaves
1 1/2 cups Arborio rice
3/4 cup white wine
1/2 cup asparagus pieces (cut diagonally
    into 1 1/2-inch lengths)
1/4 cup fresh or frozen peas
1 teaspoon lemon zest
1 tablespoon chopped fresh basil
1/4 cup chopped fresh parsley
1/4 teaspoon black pepper

Either soak saffron in stock overnight or warm
simmer in stock for 30 minutes to release its color
and flavor.

To make the risotto, warm the saffron stock in a
pot on the stove and keep to the side.

Heat Earth Balance in a thick-bottomed pot or
large sauté pan over medium heat. Add the onions
and garlic and sauté until onions just begin to
caramelize. Add dry basil, thyme sprigs, salt, and
bay leaves and continue to sauté for 1 minute.
Add the rice and stir just until rice starts to brown
on the edges and beings to pop and crackle. Add
wine and stir for 1 minute. Add warm saffron
stock, 1 cup at a time, stirring continuously.

Remove the thyme sprigs. Cook uncovered, stirring often until most of the water is absorbed and
the rice is slightly thickened and creamy. Add the
asparagus and peas and simmer, covered, until
asparagus and peas are tender. If the rice is too
thick, stir in a little stock or water. Stir in the lemon
zest and black pepper. Serve immediately.

# spinach and swiss chard with pine nuts

*Serves 4*

2 tablespoons extra virgin olive oil
2 small shallots or 3 cloves of garlic, minced
4 cups chopped Swiss chard
8 cups baby spinach
1/4 cup toasted pine nuts
1/4 teaspoon sea salt

Heat oil in a large sauté pan over medium heat.
Add the shallots (or garlic, if using) and sauté until
translucent. Add the Swiss chard and sauté for 2
minutes. Add spinach and stir until wilted. Stir in the
toasted pine nuts and a pinch of salt. Serve hot.

# white bean spread

*Makes about 1 1/2 cups*

1 15.5-ounce can navy beans
1/2 teaspoon paprika
2 tablespoons extra virgin olive oil
1/2 teaspoon sea salt
1/4 teaspoon black pepper
1 1/2 teaspoons fresh lemon juice
1 teaspoon sweet white miso
1 1/2 teaspoons chopped fresh rosemary
3 cloves roasted garlic, mashed

Drain the beans, reserving the liquid.

Place the drained beans and remaining ingredients in the bowl of a food processor. Purée until
smooth, adding bean liquid as needed to create
your desired consistency. Serve with crostini or as
a dip for vegetables.

# romesco

*Makes about 1 cup*

1 red bell pepper
2 plum tomatoes
3 cloves garlic, unpeeled
2 tablespoons extra virgin olive oil
1/3 to 1/2 cup toasted almonds
2 teaspoons balsamic vinegar
1/2 teaspoon sea salt
Pinch of black pepper
1/2 cup toasted whole-grain bread
    cubes (optional)

Toss the red pepper, tomatoes, and garlic with 1 tablespoon of the oil and a pinch of salt and pepper. Place in a baking pan and roast at 400 degrees until the pepper is charred and the tomatoes and garlic have softened, about 15 minutes. Remove from oven and cover with plastic wrap until cool enough to handle, about 10 minutes. Pour off any oil and liquid from the baking pan and reserve. Remove the skin and seeds from the pepper and tomatoes and the skin from the garlic.

Place the almonds in the bowl of a food processor. Pulse until roughly chopped. Add the toasted bread, if using, and pulse until finely ground. Add the pepper, tomatoes, garlic, vinegar, salt, and remaining oil. Puree to desired consistency, adjusting the consistency with the reserved juices.

Note: The consistency will be thinner if the bread crumbs are omitted. Serve with crostini or as a dip for vegetables.

# dinner getting saucy with pasta

**Spinach Fettucine or Rice Penne · Alfredo Sauce · Vegan Pesto Sauce · Cashew Sauce · Caponata**

*This crowd-pleasing meal is a real winner, as it satisfies a variety of dietary preferences. Whether you use a wheat-based spinach fettucine or your favorite gluten-free rice pasta, all three sauces are guarenteed to become staples in your kitchen. The traditional Italian Caponata can be served warm or cold, on the side or on toasted bread. Don't forget to add a nice big salad or some steamed broccoli to this meal.*

## spinach fettucine or rice penne

*Serves 4*

1/2–3/4 pounds spinach fettucine or rice penne

Cook pasta according to package directions. Serve hot with your choice of sauce (recipes follow).

## alfredo sauce

*Serves 4*

1 1/2 cups non-homogenized milk
2 1/2 cups heavy cream
2 tablespoons unsalted butter
2 cloves garlic, minced
1/4 cup all-purpose flour
1 1/4 teaspoons sea salt
Pinch of black pepper
1 teaspoon dry basil
1/2 cup freshly grated parmesan cheese

Heat the milk and cream in a small pot until it is just hot. Keep warm.

To make a roux, heat the butter and garlic in a sauté pan over medium-low heat. When butter is melted, slowly stir in the flour and continue to heat for 2 to 3 minutes without browning.

Slowly whisk the warm milk mixture into the roux. Stir until it has thickened slightly. Add the salt, pepper, and basil and simmer gently, stirring occasionally for 1 to 2 minutes. Stir in parmesan cheese and continue to heat until sauce becomes thick. Serve hot with pasta.

# vegan pesto sauce

*Serves 4*

1/2 cup raw almonds
1 bunch fresh basil, well-rinsed (about 2 cups)
1 cup baby spinach
3 cloves garlic
1/2 teaspoon sea salt
1/4 cup extra virgin olive oil
1/2 cup unsweetened soy milk

Place almonds in the bowl of a food processor. Puree until almonds are coarsely ground. Add basil, spinach, garlic, and salt and pulse a few times. With the motor running, slowly drizzle in the oil and blend until well combined. Transfer the pesto to a sauce pan and stir in the soy milk. Heat slowly over low heat until desired temperature is reached. Serve hot with pasta.

# cashew sauce

*Serves 4*

1 cup cashew pieces
3 1/2 cups water
1 tablespoon extra virgin olive oil
1 cup Spanish onion, medium diced
1 tablespoon chopped fresh sage
1/2 teaspoon sea salt
Pinch of black pepper
1 tablespoon chopped fresh parsley (optional)

Combine cashew pieces with water in a sauce pan. Cover and simmer for 20 minutes.

Heat oil in a sauté pan over medium heat. Add the onion and sauté until caramelized. Stir in the sage, salt, and pepper. Transfer to the pot with the cashews and simmer for 5 minutes.

Transfer onion-cashew mixture to a blender and puree until smooth. (Be careful while pureeing the hot mixture. Hold a kitchen towel over the blender lid to prevent a blow-out.) Taste and adjust seasoning with salt if desired. Garnish with chopped parsley if using. Serve hot with pasta.

# caponata

*Serves 4*

1 small unpeeled eggplant, medium diced
4 cloves garlic, minced
1 small Spanish onion, medium diced
1/2 teaspoon sea salt
2 tablespoons capers
4 plum tomatoes, chopped
2 tablespoons red wine vinegar
1 teaspoon balsamic vinegar
2 tablespoons chopped fresh basil
Pinch of black pepper

Heat oil in a skillet over medium heat. Add the eggplant, garlic, and onions and sauté for 1 minute. Add the salt and continue to sauté until onions begin to brown and eggplant is well-cooked but not mushy. At this point you can either remove vegetables from heat and let cool before adding the remaining ingredients (for a room temperature dish) or continue to sauté, adding the remaining ingredients and simmering until everything is well-combined and heated through.

# shopping for staples
Deb Morgan, chef

I love when people tell me that a recipe they learned in a program I taught at Kripalu or they found on our website is now a staple in their homes. Often, they also share that the practice of planning has become one of their most valuable tools in improving their relationship with cooking.

Here's what I recommend: Try writing down your staple meals, putting them on recipe cards, and keeping them in a file box. Then sit down once a week, and even if you just make a rough outline, say to yourself: "Okay, here are my dinners for the week," and then shop for those. That way you're not walking into the kitchen at 6:00 or 6:30 pm, thinking, "Now what do I do?" because that's daunting, and then you just go out to dinner or eat convenience foods, which are usually not the healthiest choices. A little advanced chopping of your vegetables can also go a long way.

Some staples in my household are olive oil and balsamic vinegar because I often eat in the Mediterranean style. Then I have my Asian staples: sesame oil, tamari, brown rice vinegar, garlic, and ginger. And, of course, an array of spices for Indian dishes …

With a few basics on hand, a little planning, and some favorite recipes by your side, dinner time will soon become the highlight of your day.

# dinner asian inspiration

**Tofu Young ▪ Apricot-Mustard Sauce ▪ Green Jade Vegetable Stir-Fry ▪ Summer Soba Soup**

*Tofu Young has been served for years here at Kripalu and remains a fun favorite. It is so simple to make and is delightful with our Apricot-Mustard Sauce. Serve with rice, our Green Jade Stir-Fry, and a bowl of Summer Soba soup for a quick, nutritious dinner.*

## tofu young

*Serves 4*

1 pound firm tofu, well-rinsed
1 tablespoon sesame oil
2 tablespoons tamari
1/2 cup sliced water chestnuts, drained
1/2 cup frozen peas
1/2 cup mung bean sprouts
Pinch sea salt
Oil and a little lecithin (optional but
    recommended), for wiping pan
Apricot-Mustard Sauce (recipe follows)

Place the tofu, oil, and tamari in the bowl of a food processor. Puree until tofu is smooth. Transfer to a mixing bowl. Stir in the chestnuts, peas, sprouts, and salt.

Brush a baking sheet with oil and lecithin. Use a small ice cream scoop or large spoon to scoop the tofu mixture and place on the baking sheet in patty shapes. Bake at 375 degrees for 25 minutes. Serve hot with Apricot-Mustard Sauce.

## apricot-mustard sauce

*Makes about 3 cups*

1 cup dried apricots, finely chopped
2 tablespoons minced ginger
2 tablespoons Bragg Liquid Aminos™
    (all-purpose seasoning) or tamari
1 1/2 tablespoons Dijon mustard
1/4 cup water
2 cups apricot preserves
3/4 cup orange juice
1/3 cup honey
Pinch of sea salt

Combine apricots, ginger, Bragg Liquid Aminos or tamari, mustard, and water in a sauce pot over medium heat. Cook for 10 to 15 minutes. Stir in apricot preserves, orange juice, honey, and salt. Simmer for 20 to 30 minutes until apricots are completely soft. Mixture can be served as is or blended for additional smoothness.

# green jade vegetable stir-fry

*Serves 4*

2 tablespoons sesame oil
1 cup cut green beans (about 1 1/2-inches long)
2 cups broccoli florets
2 cups chopped braising greens, such as bok choy, mustard greens, kale, or spinach
1 tablespoon minced garlic (optional)
1 tablespoon minced ginger (optional)
Sea salt, to taste
1 cup snow peas
Tamari, to taste (optional)
Toasted sesame oil, to taste (optional)

Heat 2 tablespoons sesame oil in a wok or large sauté pan over medium-high heat. Swirl oil around to coat sides of pan.

Add the green beans, stir-frying constantly for 1 minute. Add broccoli, greens, ginger, and garlic, if using, and a pinch of salt. Stir-fry until the vegetables begin to become tender. Add the snow peas and stir-fry until they are just tender, about 1 minute. Remove from heat. Serve as is or season to taste with tamari and toasted sesame oil.

# summer soba soup

*Serves 4*

6 cups vegetable stock
2 tablespoons tamari
1/4 cup sliced ginger, tied in a piece of cheesecloth
1/2 cup matchstick-cut carrots
1/4 pound soba noodles
1/4 cup sliced shitake mushrooms (stems removed)
1/2 cup matchstick-cut snow peas
1 tablespoon dried wakame seaweed
1/4 cup sliced scallions
1/2 cup watercress leaves and stems

Combine stock, tamari, ginger, and carrots in a soup pot and bring to boil. Reduce heat and simmer for 20 minutes.

In a separate pot, bring 4 cups of water to a boil. Cook the soba noodles until about 90 percent done. Remove from water and set aside.

Remove the cheesecloth bag of ginger from the broth. Add mushrooms, snow peas, wakame, and the cooked soba noodles. Cover and let sit until snow peas are tender and noodles have softened entirely. Serve hot garnished with scallions and watercress.

# seasonal specialties

# seasonal raw salads and thirst-quenching drinks

Raw Greek Kale Salad · Raw Beet and Walnut Salad · Raw Thai Salad · Hibiscus-Lavender Infusion · Moroccan Mint Tea · Basil Lemonade · Passion Punch

*Every spring and summer we add a variety of 100 percent raw salads to our already extensive salad bar and serve up some cooling drinks. While each one attracts a loyal following, the recipes below seem to get the standing ovations. The Raw Greek Kale Salad and the Moroccan Mint Tea are the favorites of many staff members and volunteers.*

## raw greek kale salad

*Serves 4*

**for the dressing**
1/3 cup extra virgin olive oil
2 tablespoons fresh lemon juice
Pinch of sea salt and black pepper

**for the salad**
4 cups shredded lacinato kale (about 1 bunch)
10 cherry or grape tomatoes, halved
8 kalamata olives, pitted and chopped
3 tablespoons pine nuts

Whisk together the dressing ingredients in a large mixing bowl. Add the tomatoes, olives, and pine nuts and toss together. Serve immediately or refrigerate.

## raw beet and walnut salad

*Serves 4*

**for the dressing**
1/4 cup extra virgin olive oil
2 tablespoons fresh lemon juice
1 tablespoon chopped fresh dill
Pinch of sea salt

**for the salad**
4 cups matchstick-cut or grated beets
1/2 cup chopped raw walnuts
1/4 cup chopped fresh parsley

Whisk together the dressing ingredients in a large mixing bowl. Add the beets, walnuts, and parsley and toss together. Serve immediately or refrigerate.

# raw thai salad

*Serves 4*

**for the dressing**

1/4 cup almond butter
3 tablespoons water
1/2 teaspoon minced ginger
1 clove garlic, minced
1 tablespoon fresh lime juice
1 1/2 tablespoons raw honey
1 teaspoon extra virgin olive oil
Pinch of cayenne (optional)
Pinch of sea salt

**for the salad**

1 cup grated carrot
1 cup shredded bok choy
1 cup finely chopped broccoli
6 radishes, thinly sliced
3 tablespoons chopped fresh cilantro

Whisk together the dressing ingredients in a large mixing bowl. Add the carrots, bok choy, broccoli, radishes and cilantro and toss together. Serve immediately or refrigerate.

# hibiscus-lavender infusion

*Makes about 2 quarts*

6 tablespoons dried hibiscus
2 tablespoons plus 1 teaspoon lavender
8 cups water
1/4 cup fresh lemon juice
1/2 cup cane sugar

Place hibiscus and lavender in a cheesecloth and tie with a string to make a pouch.

Bring water to a boil in a large pot. Turn off the heat and add the hibiscus-lavender pouch, lemon juice, and sugar. Steep for 20 minutes. Strain and chill. Serve cold.

# moroccan mint tea

*Makes about 1 1/4 quarts*

6 1/2 cups water
1/2 cup fresh mint leaves and stems, well-rinsed
3 tablespoons loose black or green tea (or 8 tea bags)
1 to 2 tablespoons sweetener such as organic sugar, honey, brown rice syrup, or agave syrup

Bring water to a boil in a medium pot. Turn off the heat, add mint, and steep for 5 minutes. Bring the mixture back to a boil. Turn off heat and add the tea. Steep for 3 minutes. Strain and sweeten to taste. Chill. Serve cold.

# basil lemonade

*Makes about 1 1/2 quarts*

1 cup sugar, plus more to taste
7 cups water
2 cups chopped fresh basil, well-rinsed
1 1/2 cups fresh lemon juice

Combine 1 cup sugar, 2 cups water, and basil in a small saucepan. Simmer until reduced by one half to make a sugar syrup. Strain into a pitcher, discarding the basil.

Add the remaining 5 cups water and lemon juice to the basil-sugar mixture. Stir well and adjust sweetness to your liking. Chill. Serve cold.

# passion punch

*Makes about 7 cups*

1 3/4 cups frozen passion fruit puree
1/4 cup sugar
5 cups water
Variety of fruit (we recommend sliced oranges, cubed plums or apples, and sliced limes)

Allow frozen puree to thaw. In a saucepan, combine sugar and 1/4 cup water and slowly heat, making a light sugar syrup. In a pitcher, add sugar syrup to thawed puree and remaining water. Add cut-up fruit and then chill. Serve over ice.

healthy living note
# food in the raw
Kathie Madonna Swift, nutritionist

Including raw-plant foods in your daily diet gives you a naturally nutrient-rich boost to better health, and summer is the best time to explore these options. Here are five quick tips for increasing your intake of raw foods:

1. Get ready for raw by investing in a few sharp knives, a wooden cutting board, and a good blender.

2. Wake up to a raw morning smoothie by tossing some apples, pears, spinach, berries, avocado, and raw almond butter in a blender with water. Yum!

3. Invite some nutrient-rich greens to your lunch by enjoying a salad made with watercress, arugula, endive, and cilantro; sprinkle with pumpkin seeds and walnuts, and dress with extra virgin olive oil, fresh lemon juice, and chopped basil.

4. Munch on a piece of fresh, seasonal fruit for a sweet afternoon treat.

5. Try a nori roll loaded with grated carrots, radishes, cucumbers, green onions, avocado, and ginger slices.

You may also want to consider freezing berries for your winter smoothies!

# seasonal delicious desserts

**Peach Raspberry Crumble • Vegan Chocolate-Cherry Cake • Maple-Sweetened Whipped Cream • Sweet Vegan Cashew Cream • Raw Coconut-Lime "Cheesecake"**

*When our magnificent bakers think of spring and summer desserts, only one word comes to mind: fruit! The Peach Raspberry Crumble is one of those wonderfully versatile desserts. Make it with fresh fruit, frozen fruit, or a combination, and then eat it warm right out of the oven or chilled. Add your favorite frozen dessert for an extra treat. And what's a better combination than fruit and chocolate? Our Vegan Chocolate-Cherry Cake is rich and delicious and vegan—unless you top it with whipped cream—as we did for the photo! And for a unique bake-free dessert, try the Raw Coconut-Lime "Cheesecake." We serve ours topped with fresh strawberries or lime and toasted coconut.*

## peach raspberry crumble

*Serves 6–8*

**for the filling**
8 cups sliced peaches (fresh or frozen, thawed)
4 cups raspberries (fresh or frozen, thawed)
1 cup honey
1 teaspoon fresh minced ginger

**for the crumble**
1/2 cup all-purpose flour
2 tablespoons whole wheat pastry flour
1/4 cup sugar
1 cup old-fashioned rolled oats
1/4 teaspoon sea salt
1/2 teaspoon baking powder
1/2 teaspoon ground ginger
1 cup chopped walnuts
1/2 cup non-hydrogenated palm shortening
3 tablespoons unsweetened soy milk

Preheat oven to 400 degrees. In a large bowl, combine peaches, raspberries, honey, and ginger and mix well. Pour into a 9x13 inch baking dish and set aside.

In another large bowl, combine dry ingredients and cut in shortening with a fork until small crumbs form. Add soy milk and keep cutting with a fork to mix to form slightly larger crumbs. Be careful not to over mix or it will resemble cookie dough. If this happens simply chop mixture with a fork to make crumbs. Sprinkle over fruit to cover most of it. Bake until golden brown on top, about 20 minutes. Serve hot, at room temperature, or chilled.

# vegan chocolate-cherry cake

*Makes an 8-inch square or round cake layer**

1/4 cup sunflower oil
1/4 cup maple syrup
1 1/2 cups unsweetened soy milk
1 tablespoon apple cider vinegar
1/2 teaspoon vanilla
3/4–1 cup sucanat or other light brown sugar
2 1/4 cups barley flour
1/2 cup cocoa powder
1/2 teaspoon baking soda
1 teaspoon baking powder
1/2 teaspoon cinnamon
1 teaspoon sea salt
1 can, drained, pitted sweet or tart cherries or
   2 cups pitted fresh sweet cherries

Preheat oven to 350 degrees. Oil a 8 x 8 baking pan or 9 inch cake pan. Combine the wet ingredients in a medium bowl. Combine the dry ingredients in a large mixing bowl. Slowly stir the wet ingredients into the dry ingredients until a smooth batter forms. Pour into an oiled baking pan or cake pan.

Drop cherries into cake batter—make sure to leave space between cherries. Bake until a toothpick comes out clean, about 35 minutes. Cool cake in pan for 5 minutes before removing. Serve with Sweet Vegan Cashew Cream or Maple-Sweetened Whipped Cream (recipes follow).

*The recipe may be doubled to make a 2-layer cake. Fill the layers and frost the tops and sides with Maple-Sweetened Whipped Cream or Sweet Vegan Cashew Cream.

# maple-sweetened whipped cream

*Makes about 3 cups*

2 cups heavy cream
1/4 cup maple syrup, or to taste
1 tablespoon vanilla

Combine the cream, syrup, and vanilla in a large mixing bowl. Use a whisk or electric mixer to whip the cream until soft peaks form. Use immediately or refrigerate and use within 4 hours.

# sweet vegan cashew cream

*Makes about 4 cups*

3 cups raw cashew pieces
1 cup water
1/4 cup agave or maple syrup
1 tablespoon vanilla

Place cashew pieces in a medium bowl and cover with the water. Soak overnight in the refrigerator.

Drain the cashews and rinse with fresh water. Place in blender with the agave or maple syrup and the vanilla. Puree until smooth and creamy (you shouldn't be able to detect any lumps from the cashews). Use immediately or refrigerate and use within 2 days.

# raw coconut-lime "cheesecake"

*Makes a 9-inch round cake*

### for the crust
1 1/2 cups raw almonds
1/2 cup unsweetened shredded coconut
3/4 cup pitted, chopped dates
1/4 teaspoon vanilla
Pinch of sea salt

### for the filling
3 cups cashew pieces
1 1/2 cups coconut milk
1 cup lime juice
3/4 agave or maple syrup (agave's raw, maple
    syrup isn't but some use it anyway)
2 teaspoons vanilla
Pinch of sea salt
3/4 cup coconut oil
3 tablespoons lecithin
Fresh berries for garnish (optional)
Toasted coconut for garnish (optional)
Lime zest for garnish (optional)

Place cashew pieces in a medium bowl and cover with water. Soak overnight in the refrigerator.

Place the crust ingredients in the bowl of a food processor. Pulse until they become crushed enough so they stay together when pinched.

Oil a 9-inch spring form pan or 9-inch pie pan and press filling into the bottom of the pan.

Combine coconut milk, lime juice, maple syrup, vanilla, and salt in a medium bowl or measuring cup. Set aside.

Drain and rinse the soaked cashews. Place in the bowl of a food processor and puree until they start to become smooth. With the motor running, slowly add the coconut milk mixture and blend until smooth. With the motor running, slowly add the lecithin and coconut oil and blend until smooth. For silkiest texture, pour half of this mixture into a blender and puree until silky smooth. Pour over crust. Repeat with the rest of the mixture. Smooth out filling with spatula and chill overnight. Pour over crust and chill overnight. If using spring form pan, remove ring before serving. Serve slices of the chilled "cheesecake" with fresh berries, toasted coconut, or lime zest if desired.

# index

Find recipe titles on page 3.

**Marketing & Communicatons**
David Surrenda, Ph.D.,
   Chief Executive Officer
Tom Rocco, Vice President,
   Marketing and Communications
Elena Erber, Creative Director
Erin Graham, Editorial Director
Joyce Monaco, Operations Manager
Derek Hansen, Graphic Designer
Ashley Winseck, Editor
Ginger Nicholson, Graphic Designer
Jonathan Ambar, Editor
Brenda Elling, Marketing Analyst
Lisa Pletzer, Web Content Coordinator
Lyn Meczywor, Marketing Assistant

**Special thanks to**
Jennifer May, Photographer
Jessica Bard, Food Stylist and
   Recipe Editor
Christine Lindemer, Indexer
Karen Moisuk, Proofreader
Qualprint, Pittsfield, Massachusetts

*Bon appétit.*

♻ Printed on recycled paper using
soy-based inks.